Chuck Zamora's

Little Black Book of
Quotes

PROFESSIONAL SUCCESS PRESS
MADISON, WISCONSIN

Copyright © 2007 by Chuck Zamora
All rights reserved.

Published by
Professional Success Press
6401 Odana Road, Suite B
Madison, WI 53719
Toll-free: 888-670-BOOK (2665)
www.professionalsuccesspress.com

Quantity discounts available for educational and charitable organizations.

ISBN: 978-1-59598-065-6
Library of Congress Number: 2007934688

Cover design by
David Paulmann Design LLC

Printed in the United States of America.

*To my parents,
Rose and Abie Zamora,
for their wisdom, counsel, and faith.
Thank you
for always being "my rock."*

Preface

Over the decades as an international professional speaker and educator, I have provided clients and friends with a "Quote of the Week," often scrounging around for days to find some piece of wisdom I felt was worth passing on. One day, while preparing for an upcoming sales training workshop, I wrote "You only have to be marginally different to be exceptional."

My personal assistant, Aleda Robbins, suggested that I use that short statement rather than continuing to look for insights and inspirations from someone else. From then on, I started jotting down my thoughts as they came to me in different situations. I also looked back through my workshop and presentation materials to gather sayings I had used to convey ideas and support actions.

Each quote has a story, a reason behind its emergence. Let me share just one with you here: I was heading down to the Gold Coast in Melbourne, Australia, for an important meeting.

Traffic was heavy and I was in a rush. In a perfect world, all of those drivers would simply have moved over and let me pass. Suddenly, a large, black Mercedes Benz flew by me in the express lane, which one could only use if one had a passenger. I knew that driver would arrive at his destination before I arrived at mine--simply because he had a passenger. As it was, I arrived at my meeting on time and took a moment to jot down this thought:

> On the highway of life, leaders always travel in the express lane because they know the fastest way to their destination is to take someone with them.

It became that week's Quote of the Week.

Here, I would like to offer some of the best quotes shared with thousands of people all over the globe through the years. My wish for this "little black book" is that some of the quotes will inspire you, perhaps some will make you stop and think, and yet others will evoke a smile or even a chuckle.

Enjoy the journey!

Early in life money is important;
Late in life memories are important.

Early in life there is chaos;
Late in life there is harmony.

Early in life we want to get;
Late in life we want to give.

Early in life it's about me;
Late in life it's about you.

Early in life rights rule;
Late in life responsibility rules.

Early in life we think we are bullet-proof;
Late in life we know we're not.

JOY *versus* **HAPPINESS**

$\mathscr{S}$eek joy over happiness. Happiness by definition requires something to happen. Joy, on the other hand, is a spirit that dwells inside all of us.

$\mathscr{L}$ook hard enough and you will find it. It will never be found in the glitz and glitter of life, but in those quiet still moments that are totally free.

On the road to success, your belief that you will succeed, will get you further than talent and drive.

For talent and drive are not enough.

But talent and drive, coupled with optimistic expectations, are almost unbeatable.

Why should we embrace failure?

Because success is a poor professor.

The biggest WRONG in business is to wait for everything to be RIGHT before you take action.

On the journey of life, obstructions are the sign posts that allow us to stop, think, and make corrections as we pursue a life that is purposeful.

*L*ove unites when all is untied, for true love requires freedom, not possessiveness.

The behaviour of a subordinate is a reflection of the leader, or of a behaviour that the leader accepts or tolerates.

Your degree of leadership will be measured by the degree of loyalty you receive from those who follow.

Sales people are hunters and gatherers—they hunt down the suspects to gather in the prospects.

From prospects, they gather information and hunt for the need.

They satisfy the need and gather in the clients.

See! They really are hunters and gatherers!

If

"WISHING and HOPING" were an effective strategy for success, the world would be inundated with successful people.

Achieving your goals should be like driving in a dense fog.

In a dense fog you can't see to the right or left nor far out front, so you stay focused on one white line at a time.

The journey may have many turns, twists and bends, and so will your goals.

But when you're forced to stay focused, those turns and twists seem to disappear.

*I*n sales, seek never to impress but always to make an impression.

To doubt is simple, but doubters are seldom doers.

To do is many times not Simple.

That's why doers never let doubt in, for they know doubt is the biggest killer of progress.

Time is limited. We only have 24 hours each day, and when that day is over, it's over.

On the other hand, money is abundant.

To put time and money into their proper perspective, we must cherish time, as it is limited, and develop a healthy respect for money.

Spending all of your time trying to make money places money above time.

The goals are not just profit, but prosperity and freedom, to maximize and enjoy every day.

Seek security and you will
   forfeit some freedom.

Seek freedom and you will
   forfeit some security.

But seek them both we must.

True freedom and true
   security are found deep
inside our beings.

The greatest security
   and the ultimate freedom
is knowing who you are.

Sight allows you to see what is.

Vision allows you to see what can be.

Complex, sophisticated technologies should be used for complex, sophisticated problems.

In most cases, common sense will do just fine.

In life and in business, the biggest risk is to never be willing to take a risk.

We're all in the game of
LIFE, and just playing is
not good enough.

You must have the desire,
Discipline, and dedication
to win...for just playing does not pay!

*I*n business,
welcome Opposition—

*J*ust don't let it become
Competition.

Physical strength makes you strong.

Emotional strength makes you tough.

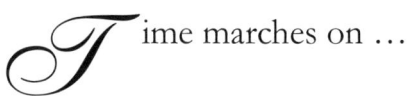ime marches on …

...so get in step.

It is tough to see the future if you are blinded by the Present.

We hear people say "you've got to think outside of the box."

I'd be happy if most would just think while they are *inside* the box!

If there is a "SHORT CUT" to success, it is to show others the way and be a leader they are willing to follow.

*I*f you want your life to be filled with joy, fill your life with service.

*F*or when you seek service, you find joy.

If you want to be a great conversationalist, learn to talk less, listen more, and ask good questions

Don't try to make life fair
because it isn't.

Try instead to make life
right for you and those
you touch.

If you want to be a "class act," let others be the stars.

*N*ever confuse confidence with arrogance.

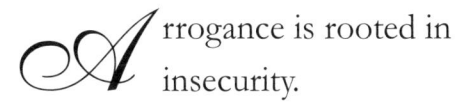

*A*rrogance is rooted in insecurity.

*C*onfidence is found in self-assurance.

A team player knows that if he lets others shine, the whole team will beam.

Old Thinking

You need to take time to sharpen the saw, which implies that the saw gets dull.

New Thinking

The saw needs to be razor sharp every day, or someone else will chop down your forest.

To ride the wave of success, you must be willing to paddle some unchartered waters ...

... Doing what others won't do;
... Going where others won't go.

What drives great sales results are the things the prospect can't see.

Never seek to be flawless;
seek to be true.

For a kite to fly higher, you cannot just let out more string. You must pull on the string and create resistance, and that resistance will lift the kite's altitude.

We must all be aware that life is many times like a kite. The resistance we can sometimes experience will be the force that has us soaring to great heights.

One of society's biggest mistakes is confusing "achievement" with "success."

Success has nothing to do with being first to the post, nor is it position or possession.

Rather, success is knowing that the lives of others are better because of what we do.

*A*t today's hectic pace, days, weeks and years can become blurred.

*M*emorable moments are crystal clear and can last a lifetime.

*S*eek to create memorable moments with those who are important to you.

There are times in your life when you need to take a stand.

Experience shows that when you take a stand, you are less likely to fall.

*W*e will always learn more about someone when we disagree.

*W*hen disagreement occurs, character is disclosed.

*S*o as a leader respect those who challenge you and your ways.

If you search for happiness you will search in vain.

Stop searching for happiness and search for a purpose.

For true happiness will be found inside your clearly defined purpose.

On the Freeway of Life, leaders always drive in the Express Lane because they know the fastest way to get to their destination is to take someone with them.

*I*t is only when you can empty your personal baggage that you will serve other well.

*F*or when you are "full of yourself" it is hard to be a servant.

Great leaders are not great because of their vision, their motivation, their inspiration, their dedication, or their drive.

Great leaders are great because of their systems and their adherence to those systems.

When a relationship breaks, it's what you do with the pieces that determines whether it's broke.

*G*reat leaders first worked leader-ship into their lives,

*T*hen let leadership work through their lives,

*K*nowing that the job was not complete until they transferred leadership to the lives of others.

Neither in sport or business does anyone ever become a top dog by being the hot dog.

In fact, most of us appreciate the quiet achiever.

*L*eadership is not achieved by way of doing certain things.

*I*t is achieved by doing things a certain way.

A broken relationship (personal or professional) is like a puzzle in a box.

The picture on the outside is a far cry from what you see inside,

But by working with each piece carefully, you can put it back together,

And be whole again.

*G*reat customer service is knowing how to "go out of the way" while never "getting in the way."

*D*issatisfaction is the precursor to either destruction or construction…

*T*he choice is always yours.

For work to be FUN, you need to be:

*F*ocused on a goal,

*U*nited as a team, and

*N*urtured by the leaders.

Corporate values have no value unless they are lived.

*B*ehavior is the outward expression of our inward appearance.

Adversity is where you learn what you cannot learn at a university.

A dollar wisely invested will increase in value.

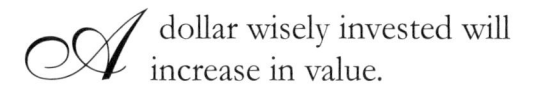

A good thought wisely invested will increase *your* value.

Sometimes we can only find faith…

When we lose everything.

We hire Subjectively,

We fire Objectively.

Great leaders know that their job is more then showing the way.

Their job is to be a light that shines, letting others find the way.

One of the best reasons to climb the corporate ladder

Is so that you can reach down and help someone up.

Being wise ...

Is to admit your weaknesses.

It is only then that great change can occur.

Those who watch the clock
Fail to see opportunities.

Those who don't watch the
clock, watch work disappear
and capture opportunities.

They are the ones who are
amazed at how time flies.

Business is like bubble gum.

It GROWS best with constant and consistent PRESSURE.

*I*f hard work were the answer to success, the world would be filled with successful people.

*S*uccess is built by thinking and acting with integrity, intensity, and purpose.

In building a great business,
It is wise to know

That growing it strong,
is better than growing it fast,

For many times, fast won't last.

*I*n business, always choose the BATTLE ZONE over your COMFORT ZONE.

*F*or like the butterfly, it is the struggle to get free from the cocoon that gives it the strength to fly.

*L*ife is more abundant when we place greater value on SELF-WORTH then we do on NET WORTH.

*U*nderstand that things don't happen to us in life, but rather we happen to things.

*H*ow we do that, will greatly determine the kind of life we lead.

*L*ife consists of thousands of problems, dilemmas, AND challenges, where choices must be made.

*T*he goal is to be aware that RESOLVE should never override RIGHT.

*In building your life,
the best foundation is love.*

Know that money matters.

But in pursuit of making money, don't forget to make memories.

For there comes a time in our lives when the bank account called MEMORIES will be our greatest ASSET.

Small incremental changes in behavior create LARGE, long-term sustainable growth.

The ultimate in success is when happiness and achievement converge.

Life is like a merry-go-round. You can sit on the side and watch it go around, or you can get on and enjoy the ride.

The choice is yours.

*S*etting a goal is
   IMPORTANT,

*H*aving it time-framed is
   CRITICAL,

*N*ot accepting the
   consequences of failure
is VITAL.

Desire, commitment, and drive must be underpinned by integrity, faith, and fairness for sustainable success to be achieved.

The Challenge in learning is not what is taught, it's what is caught.

So put on your catcher's mitt and make learning a life-long passion.

You can **DREAM** about success, but it takes a **TEAM** to achieve it.

*I*t maybe easy to hide the flames of dishonesty, but it is much harder to hide the smoke.

*T*herefore, in this case, the axiom "where there is smoke, there is fire" just might be true.

One of the great keys to listening is to accurately interpret what wasn't said.

Building a great product is essential.

Caring for your customers so they will come back and buy more, is vital.

If someone comes to you with the SECRETS of Success—RUN! (there are no secrets)

If someone wants to teach you the truths about success, BE A STUDENT.

If you run your business on values,

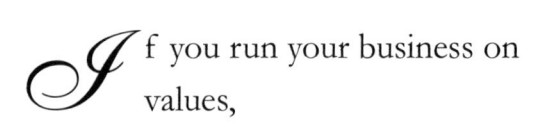

*R*ules become redundant.

Knocking on doors is easy.

Knowing what to do if someone answers could be a little more difficult.

Your OUTlook in life is greatly determined by what you see when you look INside.

To be self-assured and proud
is the kind of human music
that is **NEVER** loud.

Selling Mistake #1: Information overload.

The smart salesperson knows that the goal is to sell today.

You will always have time to educate tomorrow.

Leading without loyalty is like taking a walk alone.

What *you* were—you were.

What you are—you are.

What you will be
Is yet to be determined.

SALES TIP!!!
Don't take a "NO" from someone who can't say "YES"!

Go to the top for your answers.

Customer Service is:

Satisfying customers' wants, needs, and desires, as well as exceeding their expectations.

Through quality product, workmanship, and on-time delivery, creating a memorable experience and making price a secondary issue.

To view a mistake as a mistake is a mistake.

All mistakes should be viewed as learning experiences.

Rule of Thumb:

You will always sell more when you stop trying to sell your product and instead sell yourself and your ability to satisfy your customer's wants, needs, and desires.

Life is a classroom that gives tests daily.

"ACME"

Always
Create a
Memorable
Experience

A Customer Service Philosophy ...

Don't burn your bridges,

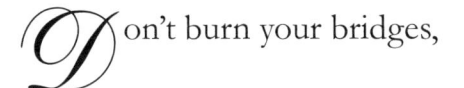

Build them!

*I*f you desire to **SUCCEED**, you will find a way.

*T*he fear is to **NOT SUCCEED** and make excuses.

Selling = Helping

Helping = Caring

Caring = Giving

When you learn to **GIVE**, you will **SELL MORE**.

As a **LEADER**, you are ultimately in charge.

When you know, you can let go.

A folly of life is that we tend to stretch the imagination as to what we can do in a year and fall grossly fall short of what we could accomplish in five.

When you look at the bright side of life, you'll never need sunglasses.

*L*ive your life frame by frame but always focus on the big picture.

Don't tell your customers how good you are. Show them!!

Good looks can open doors.

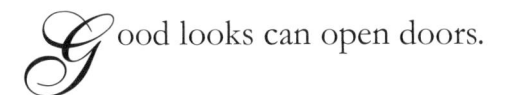

Being good gets you in.

Delivering the goods creates long-term success.

Failure does not exist for people who have not lost their courage, their character, their self-respect, or their self-confidence.

They are still champions in life experiencing a setback.

*I*t is your programming that has created your choices in the past.

*I*t is the choices you make today that are creating the program of your future.

The question is not "How much does this person work?" but rather "How much does this person accomplish?"

*L*earn how to SEE with your EARS ("I see what you mean") and

*L*ISTEN with your EYES (The visual message is a powerful communicator)

When you finally know you're on the right road,

It becomes the highway to your success.

When all else fails, go back to the basics.

They will never let you down.

If sales and marketing are not the steering wheel of your business, you won't drive it very far.

You only need to be marginally different to be successful.

Success is not the essence of failure.

Success is the accumulation of knowledge gained from failure applied.

About the Author

Chuck Zamora has been sharing his expertise in customer service, sales, and personal development for over four decades. Recognized in Australia as one of the top providers of on-site and public seminars, Chuck has earned a reputation for obtaining maximum performance from people and businesses.

Chuck is a devoted corporate trainer and through Zamora Training, founded in 1984, has been providing seminars to organizations of all sizes on leadership, goal-setting, negotiation, and interpersonal skills. His flagship presentations include "The Art of Conversational Selling" and "Corporate Leadership and Success Strategies" (CLASS).

As a highly respected keynote speaker, Chuck is frequently invited to deliver entertaining and provocative addresses to corporations and professional associations.

Prior to his corporate training career, Chuck received degrees in Education and Social Sciences from San Diego State University. He worked for nearly a decade in both the United States and Australian educational systems, where he not only taught but was responsible for developing strategies in cooperative teaching practices.

Before returning to the United States after living in Australia for more than thirty years, Chuck addressed over 10,000 senior high school students annually through his "Developing Personal Performance" program, which involves workshops on communication, attitude and self-image, goal-setting, problem-solving, and leadership.

Please visit www.zamoratraining.com for more information on Chuck's dynamic and effective presentations, keynotes, and in-house corporate seminars.